DEC - - 2007

POEMS IN BLACK & WHITE

Library of Congress Cataloging-in-Publication Data
Miller, Kate.
Poems in black and white / by Kate Miller.
p. cm.
ISBN-13: 978-1-59078-412-9 (alk. paper)
1. Children's poetry, American. I. Title.
PS3613.I5394P64 2006
811'.6—dc22
2006011844

WORDSONG
An Imprint of Boyds Mills Press, Inc.
A Highlights Company

815 Church Street
Honesdale, Pennsylvania 18431

POEMS IN

BLACK&WHITE

Kate Miller

WORDSONG
HONESDALE, PENNSYLVANIA

For
my twin treasures
Ben and Luke

and

in memory of my brothers
Ralph and Jim

CONTENTS

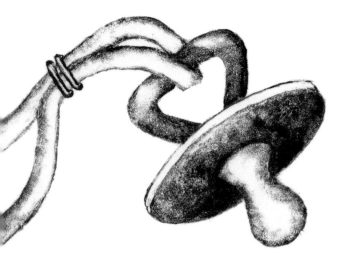

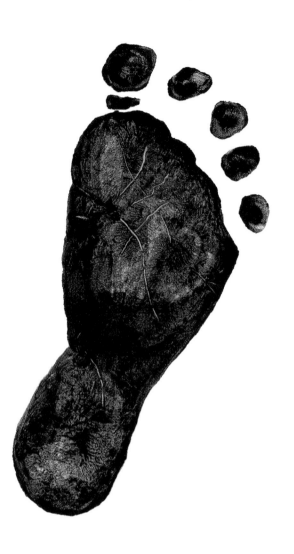

FIRST STEPS

when you were new
just minutes old
and baby bare
they caught your
pedaling feet
just long enough
to ink them black
and press their prints
upon a glossy sheet
of pearl-white paper

two tapered soles
of elfin size
creased with lines
unique to you that
mark you mine
ten rounded toes
like stepping stones
left and right
a perfect pair
adventure bound

COMET

A swirling smudge
    of luminescent white
it flings a dusty tail
    of blurry light
  across
the neatly ordered sky—
  a tease
    of breezy
      imperfection—
        as if some
          impish thumb
            had smeared
            a star
              before
                the night
                  had dried

DAD'S CLOSET

pried off and
roughly tossed
into the clutter
of fishing gear
and garden tools
Dad's shoes lie
sidewise on the
closet floor
their heel backs
flattened by
impatient feet
that have no use
for tiresome laces
the black leather
scuffed and torn
from stolen
hikes he took
(with me in tow)
through weeds
and underbrush
in search of
wildflowers

on a crooked hook
hangs his rumpled
doctor's coat and in
the pocket a steely
stethoscope and sprig
of pussy willow

A FLY IN FEBRUARY

A streaking
zinging
speck
of tar-black
frenzy
ricochets 'round
whitewashed walls
to find the
spot
from which it crept
too early
or
too late
but now forgot.

What insect fate
awaits
this noisy
lace-winged
dot?

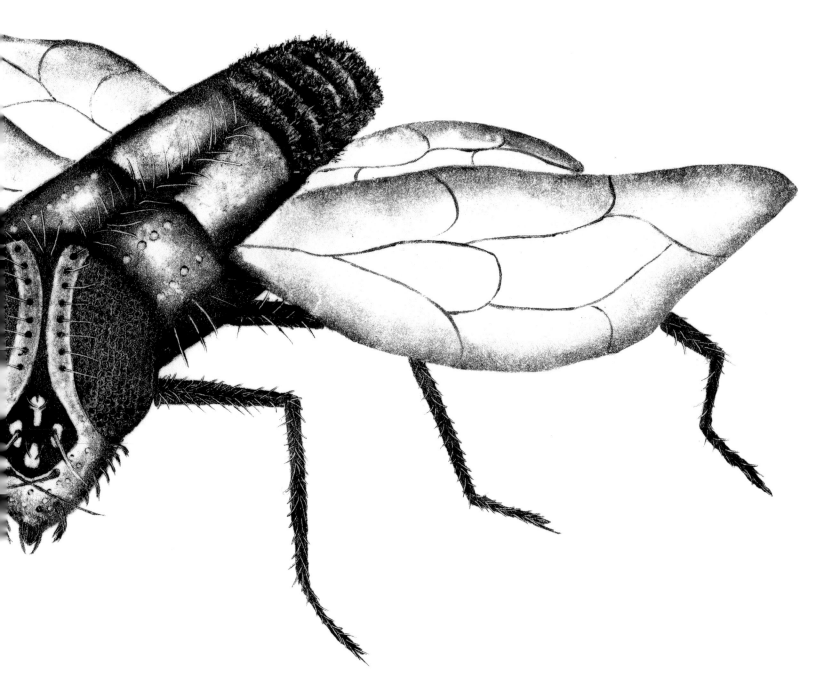

MISS FITZGIBBON'S BOARD

Squint
And you might see
The outlines of
A blackboard memory
Preserved in molecules of chalk
Embedded in the slate
Some sixty years ago
A ghostly penance
Scribbled hastily
By some naughty
Student of the past
Not once—
But several hundred times:

"I must not talk in English class."

Math Homework
Read pages 30-40
Answer questions 1-10

Haiku — 17 syllables

"New Year's Day"
The earth rolls over (5)
Stretches its stiffened limbs and (7)
waits for winter's end (5)

$$\frac{3}{5} \div \frac{3}{4} = \frac{\cancel{3}}{5} \times \frac{4}{\cancel{3}} = \frac{4}{5}$$

Mercury
Venus
Earth
Mars
Jupiter
Saturn
Uranus
Neptune
Pluto

Play Practice
7:00 PM
Thursday

CURTAIN CALL

Aunt Lima's cat
slinks along the
narrow sill parting
the white lace drapes
of crocheted roses
and scattered vines
so she can bask in
the flattering spotlight
of noon-day sun that
makes her black fur
glimmer like a diva's
sequined gown.

Somewhere in this
waking dream she
hears the sound of
grateful applause
then curves her tail
into a swanlike S
and gracefully lowers
her head and chest
as if to bow
(but not humbly)
to her adoring
audience.

DANDELION DREAMS

the dandelion is
a fuddy-duddy—
a stick-in-the-mud
whose long stubborn
root anchors her safely
to the familiar earth

but above the ground
her head is filled with
winged seeds—her fluffy
cloud-white dreams held
back like eager children
until they're ripe enough
to leave upon the next
unscheduled breeze

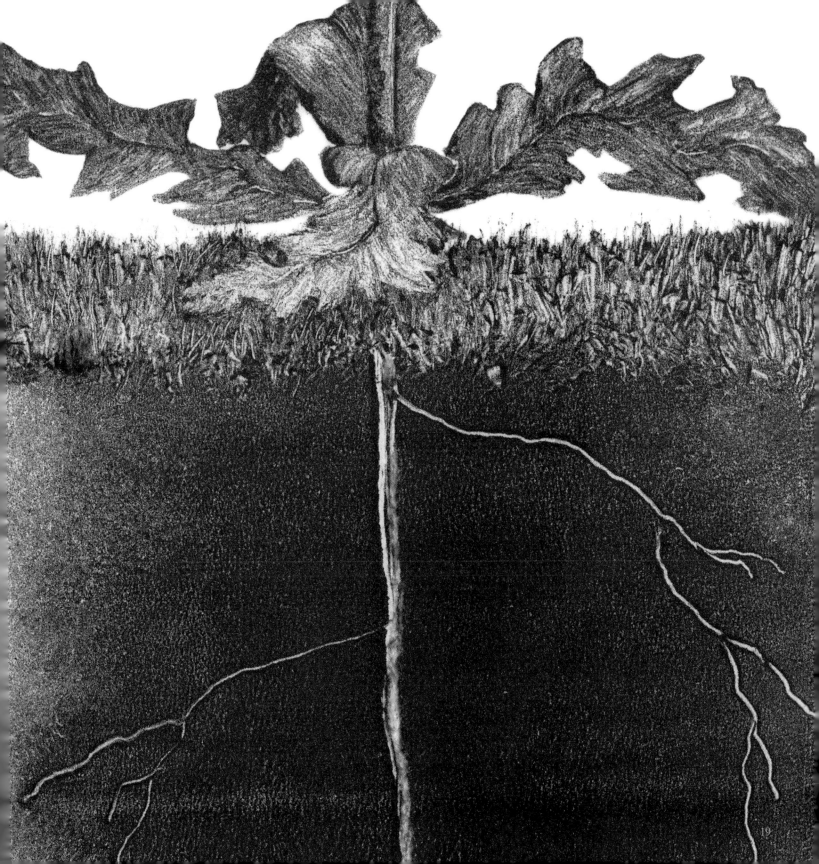

DOG-EYED

A canine's sight is
black and white.
Within his eyes
no color lies—
no rhubarb red
or cat's-eye green
or even butter yellow.
Light and dark
and shades of gray
are all he recognizes.
From dog-eyed views
a rainbow's hues are
simply drab and
boring.

So when my dog is
feeling plain
or ordinary
I pat him on
his troubled head
and gently
reassure him
that among
his doggy friends
his Border Collie
black and white
is just as grand as
Irish Setter red.

POPCORN

How marvelous
it is that from
these homely
bashful seeds

crunchy
            cratered
snow-white blossoms
                burst noisily
and gratefully
            shout

POP! POP! POP!

to those who set them free!

ALMOST PERFECT

Grandfather wears
a long-sleeved shirt
with buttons fastened
trimly to his neck
barely a whisper
of wrist peeking
gentlemanly from
starched white cuffs
not a single wrinkle
disrupts the neatness
of the look

but there's an
inkling of rebellion
where the triangular
points of his collar
curl up in defiance
of the iron's press
and in the haphazard
medley of crinkles
that bloom like weeds
at the edges of his
roguish eyes

THE COW

Because
she wears
a bristly map
of milkweed white
and midnight black

it seems
as though
she's
strong enough
to carry continents
upon her back

with oceans
in between

and   islands   on her
knees

MY MOTHER'S HAIR

my mother's hair
is satin black
except for one small
patch of white—
a single rose afloat
on wind-tossed waves
in a silky onyx sea—
a prophecy of
what's to come when
she's no longer young

RACCOON IN WINTER

Within
thin splinters
of raw moonlight
the dog spies
the blackness
that is your furry guise.

Only he can see
the white around
your bandit eyes
or hear the
scented sound
of thieving paws.

He barks
he growls
he sniffs the ground
and prowls
the hazy darkness
with his gaze.

We wonder at
the cause of
all his raucous show—
all *we* see is
night and
snow.

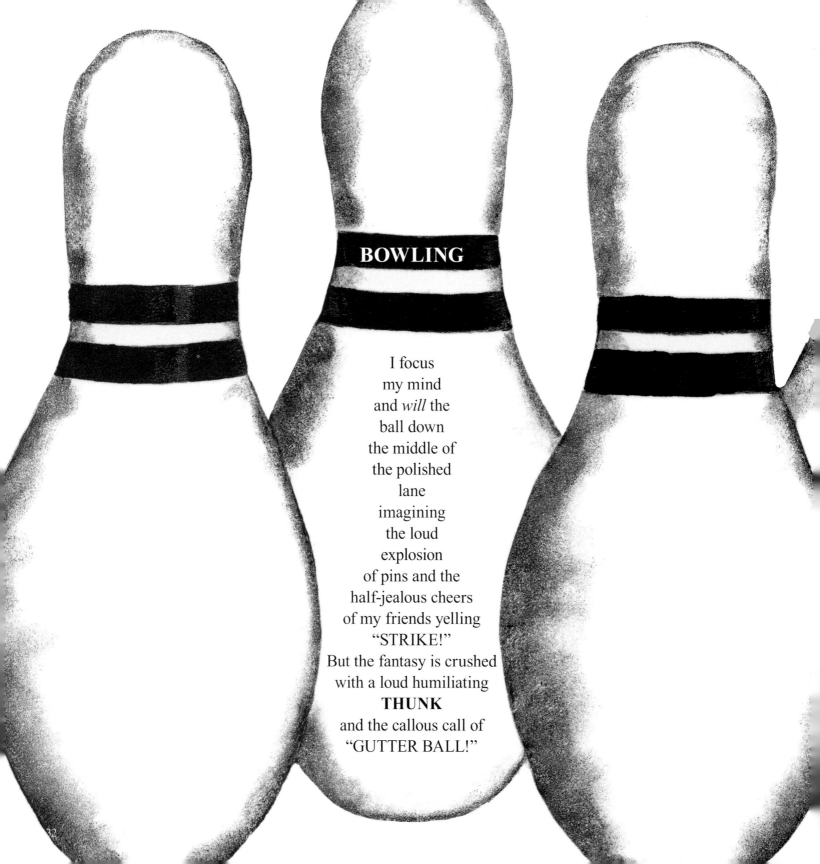

BOWLING

I focus
my mind
and *will* the
ball down
the middle of
the polished
lane
imagining
the loud
explosion
of pins and the
half-jealous cheers
of my friends yelling
"STRIKE!"
But the fantasy is crushed
with a loud humiliating
THUNK
and the callous call of
"GUTTER BALL!"

KING CROW

I have no
gaudy plumage
to attract
the poet's eyes
or even those
of fellow crows
in flight.

Instead I wear
a feathered mirror
of sleekest black
to steal
the white-hot sun
and proudly
flash it back
as shining plumes
of rainbowed light.

I have no
drowsy melody
to charm
and hypnotize
or warbled notes
within my throat
to sing.

Instead I shriek
a homely squawk
a bossy *CAW*
to rule
this dried-up field
of brown-stalked
corn and straw
and stake my claim
as raven king.

THE TUNNEL

rain beats
our car like
a steel drum
its rhythm
fierce and
threatening

suddenly
blackness and
brief relief as

the pelting stops
and the serious
              swish
      swish
              swish
of windshield wipers
becomes a playful
              squeak
      squeak
              squeak

Who would have
thought darkness
could be so cheerful?

TIC-TAC-TOE

the sun's shy sister
waits for night to play
then sends her timid
beams of alabaster
light through friendly
fingerprinted panes

in darkened rooms
where children sleep
she casts a wavy grid—
her lonely shadow game—
pointed stars will be the X's
round planets, spinning O's

ABOUT THE ILLUSTRATIONS

To make a monotype—the kind of illustration used in this book—Kate Miller applies a slow-drying paint to Plexiglas and uses wooden sticks, her fingers, or even lace to create texture and shading. Once the painting is complete, she presses a sheet of paper onto the Plexiglas, and when she peels it off, *voilà!*: a one-of-a-kind piece of art.